Listening Still

To Vince —
    With admiration,
gratitude, and love,
        Edna

Listening Still

Poems
Edna Small

Hartley-Wildman Publishing

Published in the United States of America
by Hartley-Wildman Publishing

Library of Congress Control Number 2016901076

ISBN 978-1-63273-024-4

Cover art: Julie Small-Gamby, *Slicing Through*, 2010,
(42″ x 38″). Oil and fabric on canvas.

Author photograph: Susan Eva Small, 2015.

In memory of
Sophie Jaffe Small
Abraham Aaron Small

Contents

Shaped

A Slice of Life

i

Seasons

Listening Still

Time Shifts

Far From Home

Round About

Acknowledgements

Shaped

Race Point
(Provincetown, Massachusetts)

A fragile crop of land, a seamless ocean.
Our teenaged children who dripped crooked castles
on this beach as soon as they could toddle
to its edge, now toss a frisbee freely
in the air, race to interrupt its fall
and fling it back again; our dogs run in
and out of gently teasing waves. And I
inhale the cutting cleanness of the air.

My grandparents crossed these very waters
leaving all they knew for a new atmosphere.
The children frolic, they breathe so casually;
I so consciously take in this air that fills
my lungs, the ceaseless rhythm of the surf
that fills my ears, the vastness of the sea
that sates my eyes. I am immense and small.
Our youngsters play, their journeys yet unknown.
I taste the salt slip down my face.

Naming

In the beginning, we are told,
God created the world, then
man gave each living thing a name.

My mother's mother was married
to a man devoted to his faith.
He spent his years in study
with the men; she spent hers
carrying children, keeping house.
She served the pious man.

I did not know her, really.
She seemed worn and wan.
I shrank from her whiskered kiss,
the still air at her bedside.

The names she gave her daughters
now roll off my tongue: Venus,
Esther, Sophie, Adeline, Elizabeth,
Genevieve. What did she hope
each time she chose a name?

Her name was Ida.
I always thought her name
was Rose.

Shaped

Henri Moore's shelves held driftwood and stones,
shells and bones, his *library of shapes.*

My father's windowsills held driftwood, coral,
and pebbles, found on the beach, placed among
his potted plants, his *legacy of shapes.*

My father, an unassuming man, would have laughed
to have been called a surrealist.

Orphaned early, his life was shaped by loss,
but he shaped a garden brimming, in season:
lilac and forsythia, iris, peonies, pansies
and petunias, hollyhocks, aster, black-eyed Susan.

A mindful man, he left the papers of his life
in shape: ledgers, burial instructions, his will. He left,
as well, a legacy of love of shapes, surfaces, and depths.
And the tenderness to tease seedlings into bloom.

The Gift

I wake up in my father's arms
bouncing against his chest
as he climbs up
and up and up.
Inside the dim lobby
I scream.
There before me is
a nearly naked man
twisted on a wooden cross.
I grip my father's neck
and close my eyes again.

She's just three,
my father says,
putting me down on a narrow bed.
She'll be all right,
a strange voice says.
I peek out at a woman
all in white, a hanging hood
hiding her hair.

My bed moves. Rails appear.
Blue men and bright lights loom.
A mask clamped over my mouth and nose
makes my breath strange.
Deep sleep, and yet
I hear the saw buzz through
the bone in my right ear.

I open my eyes.
The little room is back.
My head is wrapped in white
so tight I cannot scratch.

Aunt Bea stops by.
I'll bring a gift.
What would you like?
A gun,
I say.

Unspoken

Mother's care caressed me:
brushed and plaited hair,
labored stitches for a
new red coat, chocolate-chip
cookies baking in the kitchen.

Always a plate of apples,
pears, or grapes to greet
my friends. On birthdays,
a sour cream chocolate cake.
I could swirl the batter,
lick the bowl.

What was missing? Words.
Words were always missing.
Her stories, her losses, her love
lived in silence.

I search,
poem by poem,
for the missing words.

My Father's Gardens

Pieces of driftwood and smooth sea-washed stones
adorn my father's windowsills. He found
them lying on the beach, gave them new homes
among the plants, his garden of lost ground.

At five, he loved the flowers his sister grew
in silent earth that also held the bones
of parents whom he only briefly knew.
He lined the borders with his treasured stones.

Later, his own garden greeted him each day.
He'd wash his grease-stained hands, give a kiss,
then tend to shrubs and blooms. We kids would play
or gather scattered stones his eyes had missed.

His flowers thrived, as do the plants he's grown.
No garden is complete without its stones.

Mother, Widowed

Teardrops of dawn dampen the grass
you hover in my sleep
mine brim behind still closèd lids
I never heard you weep

Alone with age, with vision dim
I see you silence fear
you heed the calling of each day
I weep your unshed tears.

Scrabbled

I have no place to put the word *content*
on the open board. You will go first.
You've made it known that this is your *intent,*

the more than ninety years that you have spent
feel quite enough—to stay would seem a curse.
But I've no place to put the word *content.*

Tiles fill the board. The rules which you invent
are those we play by—no need that we converse.
You have made known so surely your intent,

insist the words you've said are what you meant:
you've had your turn, you've lost your former thirst,
have found a place to put the word *content,*

are glad to have blank tiles as a portent.
To leave while still a player—it could be worse,
and you've made known that this is your intent.

An hour goes by as if it were a moment.
Is it the game in which we are immersed?
Though I've no place to put the word *content,*
you have. We know that this is your intent.

Geography

We are both silent.
You breathe, can
no longer speak.
Are you asleep?

I hold your hand, hope
it's of some comfort
to you as well.

My eyes map your face,
deeply etched rivers,
byways crisscrossed,
disappearing.

I smooth your strands
of hair, and sigh.
You stir,
and so do I.

And so do I.

Elegy for Jason
1973-1996

Waves pulse along the coast
cliffs sheer
the sky

how long did you
travel for this glimpse?
how long did that weak
vessel lurk within?

you watch the icy ball
travel through darkness   its tail
startles the stars

once unblinking eyes
clench shut   you have seen
a silent surge roars within

the comet gone from view

After Words

One by one, we grasp
the heavy handle,
work the shovel
into the clay, drop
clods of earth into
the opened ground.

Each time, the rabbi
takes back the shovel,
forces it upright
into the mound;
metal on gravel
punctuates the silence.

Her granddaughters,
looking down,
part with purple irises.

The Comment Book

Julie Small-Gamby, Paintings and Sculpture,
Adelphi University, November, 2002.

"It Never Entered My Thoughts,"
you titled the show.

Your work is poetry.
Strong show.
Thanks. Glad I came.
The stuff of dreams.
Generative.

To write some words
leaves so much more
unsaid. I love your work
leaves so much out.

It is you,
soft and strong,
fluid and formed,
process ... essence ... unsayable.

Seeing

I see the house we lived in
that summer years ago
when first I looked within
in ways I did not know.

That summer years ago
you, child, a gift to me
in ways I did not know
in ways I could not see.

You, my child, a gift to me
a whole new aspect to the day
in ways I could not see
your vision showed the way.

A whole new aspect to my day
a sky of gold, a ground of blue
your vision was a startling way
to see my dailyness anew.

A sky of gold, a ground of blue
winged seed-pods dancing to the ground
I saw my dailyness anew
old joys, old treasures, newly found.

Winged seed-pods dancing to the ground
I floated with them, finally free
old joys, old treasures, newly found
in ways that only I could see.

I floated with them, finally free
no longer bound by fears
in ways that only I could see
I treasured my new cares.

No longer bound by fears
when first I look within
I treasure my new cares.
It is the house I live in.

Revelation

She cut an apple
across the middle,
revealed a star.
She pried apart
a single peanut,
revealed a tiny Santa.

She showed me
a way to see.

What I Know

I don't know when it all began.
I don't know when we left the garden,
loosed the dove, or crossed the parted sea.

Before my birth I knew it all,
or so I have been told. God flicked
his finger, made me forget.

I don't know how the heavens hold the stars,
how sound rides on waves, nor how
the magic of the moon commands the surf.

I was not there the moment
of your birth, did not hear your mother's
moans, the curse God placed on Eve.

But I know the moment when my love began:
I saw you swaddled, waiting to be held,
ready to grasp my finger, and come home.

And I was there when the scalpel
sliced, gloved hands reached in
for your own fast-failing twins.

The hand of God was still.

To Susan, March 16, 2002

It is their birthday.
Morgan and Nicholas
would be five today
had they been able to thrive,
to survive in this vale of tears.
But neither science
nor your prayers
could save them for life on earth.
You gave them birth and such pure love.
They live on in your memory,
I see you watch them grow
and weep for you
for they are gone.
And your heart's not whole
yet. But know this: it never is
once such love has lived there.
It was not their time to live,
but the depth of love
you have to give is
needed in this life.
So treasure them in memory
but also love yourself.
It pains me so to see you sad
and yet I'm glad your feelings
are so deep.
Do not be afraid of loving
with your whole being
and broken heart.
Your heart, embedded with your twins,
is larger than you know.

This is your time to live.
You have so much
to give to so many.
I know your grief is heavy without measure,
more than your due,
but I treasure your breath,
your warmth, your life
and pray you'll keep on being fully you.

A Slice of Life

Aubade

My mouth furry
with the morning
I fight to curl
beneath the down
that blankets me.
My mind floats free.
I know more now

than I will know
when I rinse
sticky slumber
from my lids,
swirl mint against
my teeth and tongue,
tingle awake.

Even as I put
my glasses on
my vision fades.
Desire morphs
into doubt.
Pros and cons
confound me.
glaring screens,
staccato news,
assault me.

I have lost
silence.

A Slice of Life

A squish of juice
awakens my tongue
sluices down my throat
with the pulp of tangerine.
The edge is off my thirst
the flavor lingers.
Although I savor
each remaining piece
none is as startling
as the first.

The Cord

Yellow has burst
through winter's gloom—
crocuses, daffodils,
forsythia.

I wait for your call.

Yesterday
I noticed the grime
on my down jacket.

This morning
gray squirrels mate
on my deck railing.

I wait for your call.

I soak my jacket,
buffet it with yellow
tennis balls to dry.

Molly calls. *Can't talk,*
I tell her, cradling
the phone.

I wait for your call.

It's over, you say
through the black
cord, your voice
strangled.

Telling Time

Now, time is jerky—
intermittent. Numbers
change abruptly.
Bright red digits
jangle, tease my mind
to untangle what
15:15 means.

Then, time was smooth—
hands moved slowly
around the circle, quietly
segmenting the hour.
I miss the hands
that measured my days.
They moved with grace.

Curse

Menstruation, tears of an empty uterus.

Imagine, a weeping womb, red tears
flowing monthly since I was ten,
never nourishing life.

Surgeons stopped that flow,
removing a womb
useless in their view.

My uterus. To ancient Greeks
a seat of hysteria,
a female curse.

A greater curse would be
to not feel, on my face,
the sting of salt.

Rearrangement

```
      E   A
    R       S
  B           T
```

bare

stare

beast

tears

stab

sear

rest

bets?

Depression

I have not written
a poem
for weeks.
My pen is
broken,
dispirited,
limp.
Please erectify.

At Dawn

Bird songs
from the bamboo
beckon me from bed.
Bodies hidden, voices clear,
sparrows sing me into day.
If my voice were strong,
if I had a song,
I too could sweeten the air.

Tilting at Rainbows

It all depends
on how you tilt
your head
and where
you stand.
I have always
wanted to be
at the edge
of the rain.
I have wanted
to surprise
the arc
in the sky.
I have angled
for a glimpse
of the fabled
pot, delighting
in the game,
not the gold.

Bird Shit

On my windshield
a work of art,
minimal, abstract.
White streaks
smudged with purple,
bits of undigested berries
on the base of each stroke.
Some days I see only the shit.
Today, a wonder.

Unlisted

How long the list of things I cannot do,
new minuses are added every day.
The sun is setting and our hours are few.

I used to be so sure of what I knew,
and *Memory* was just a game to play.
How long the list of things I cannot do.

I don't hear very well—you know that's true,
I'm never sure I catch the words you say.
The sun is setting and our hours are few.

I notice that I'm walking slowly, too,
and hope my buckling knees will not give way.
How long the list of things I cannot do.

I need your arms to strengthen me anew,
your touch to tell me that I'm still okay.
The sun is setting and our hours are few.

The miracle is being here with you.
Please promise that you'll do your best to stay.
How long the list of things I cannot do.
The sun is setting and our hours are few.

Whisperings

The dear dead,
those near me in years,
or younger still,
are speaking up again.

They used to whisper
from time to time
an admonition, a warning.
Sometimes a loud *bravo*.

Now, I listen, all ears,
inner ears that pick up
vibrations, intimations,
and the urgency of *now*.

Prayer

The bamboo prays before me
swaying back and forth
like my grandfather's bearded minyan
davening in shul:
back and forth they rocked.
They kissed the sacred words
carried, covered, through
the narrow aisles.

The words, The Book.
Books beckoned me, blessed me,
brought me a world of words.
I seldom go to synagogue,
but bend and straighten
with the wind.

The Last Chapter

I rest the book,
a few pages
still to go.

I let myself drift,
not ready to leave
this other world.

My Desk

This dear desk on which I write,
three broad boards of pine gaping at the seams,
weathered skin rich with random scuffs and scratches,
fine thin lines, and darker ones more deeply etched,
edges, rough with wear, softened in spots, unstained.
Distressed is not a word I choose to use.

Knowledge

I can only
write about
what I don't know

What I know
slips like a minnow
between pen and page

Seasons

Summer Heat

A branch stirs, stills
in the weighted air.

Gnats gather at my buzzing head.
A whiff of wind, a blue-black
luminescence.

Seasons

Again I've journeyed to this special place,
First one, then two, now fifty some odd years.
A weird, migrating bird without a call
Winging my way to each surprising season.
I sit and watch the feathered birds fly by,
I see the open sky change through the day.

The tides dictate the rhythm of my day,
The clock no longer has a central place.
I'll gaze down from the high dune by and by,
Let steady waves erase the passing years.
I'm here to feel once more the change of season,
To watch the wind, to hear the crickets call.

No longer do I hope that you will call,
But treasure the unfolding of each day.
I do not need your tone or touch to season
Present time. Still, I never would replace
Those youthful summer months—for many years
I've thought of you, and of those days gone by.

Somehow we never really said goodbye.
At times I pause, aware—as I recall
Children laughing, splashing—years and years
Have been transformed into a single day.
Young ones now are claiming their own place.
I know how long it takes a life to season.

For countless years in every passing season
I've mixed the present with the days gone by.
But in this very time, this very place
I answer to a stronger, inner call.
The voice that sounds so clear and crisp today
Was faint and formless for so many years.

I have no way to count on future years:
I'll settle for this one, this treasured season,
Enjoy the pattern of each passing day.
Look up—a vee of geese is flying by,
Returning to a given place,
Responding to a timeless call.

The day, the month, the season.
How swiftly years slip by.
Still, a place calls.

On The Deck

the morning and I awaken.
The birds tune up,
some echoing each other—
surely not really mocking.
A whistled trill, a metallic *caw*.
I feast on a soft, repetitive drill,
then a chorus of call and response.
A soloist goes his own way.
Even the occasional silence
absorbs me: I listen to the air.
Overhead, a huge gull wings by.
A white-throated sparrow perches
on the top-most pine,
surveys his domain,
pours forth pure piccolo notes.
I hear the click of a noisemaker
twirling the new year in,
then a melodic medley.

A muffled motor, discordant,
shatters the surround. It retreats,
gifting me again the silent atmosphere
broken only by avian greetings.
Did I listen this intently
before my hearing began to fail?

Sunset

We drive to watch the sun set at Duck Harbor,
where western sky and bay both meet the eye.
The sun is whole, but low enough by now
to cast a glistening swath across the water.
It is low tide. Gulls skim the shallow pools.
Children, gleeful in the muck, dig and squish.
The sun dips behind the clouds, then drops
behind the horizon. We raise wine glasses
to the departing sun. The sky's alive
with tints of orange; the air turns cooler.
We leave as mottled purple hues appear.
I glance back despite the growing chill.

What Holds

Wood posts
emerge bit by bit,
single, paired, or clustered.
Slimy kelp mingled
with grass-green seaweed
clings to them. Deep crevices
are carved in the dampened wood.
The posts hold me.

Out on the exposed flats,
shell-fishermen harvest oysters,
dig for clams. Simeon returns
with his haul, stops his truck on the sand.
What are these posts? I ask.

He looks at me, pulls at his ear
They're from the old Chequesset Inn
overlooking the bay.
Winter 1934, shifting pack-ice
tore at the pilings.
They didn't hold.

What's left is what you see.

Cane In Hand

At high tide, I step cautiously
into the bay until the water
reaches my knees. I don't join
the swimmers, but inch
my way back to the beach.

I pass a young woman
sifting through the sand,
as I did for so many years.
Smiling, she offers me
the treasure cradled in her palm.

I select a small mottled stone.

Last Day

It is time to leave, almost.
The day is shorter
than yesterday.

The sun rose early.
So did I.
The steady ocean
never slept,
the moon is still clear.

The ironweed is fading,
goldenrod appears.
The white butterflies
have left the garden.
Today, I'll look
at a single stem
of Queen Anne's Lace.

I'll watch
one herring gull
tussle with a crab
at high tide.

Autumn Leaves

The autumn leaves have all but gone away
one last tall iris stiffens with the cold.
What changes wait outside my door today?

The hummingbirds are gone, the sparrows stay
squirrels scamper, surefooted and bold.
The autumn leaves have all but gone away.

Black walnut limbs are bare, the bamboo sways
the air is crisp, a chill within its hold.
What changes wait outside my door today?

The children are no longer free to play
they sit at desks and do as they are told.
The autumn leaves have all but gone away.

This season too will pass, as each new day
arises in the waning of the old.
What changes wait outside my door today?

The mirror shows my hair is turning gray
the season's turning is always foretold.
The autumn leaves have all but gone away.
What changes wait inside my door today?

bare limbed trees
in murky waters ...
the world upside down

The Bamboo

The wind is thrashing my bamboo, a swirl
of bending stalks and swishing leaves that scratch
my windowpane. For a moment they unfurl,
show the relentless wind it's met its match.

When the bamboo is weighted down by snow,
is covered with the clarity of white,
it seems to yield, bows to the ground below,
but then resumes its own majestic height.

Some days it sways and dips, a gentle dance,
some days rocks back and forth like men at prayer.
It constantly resumes an upright stance
with just a wave to greet the passing air.

Rooted wide and deep the culms hold sway,
and weather every storm that comes their way.

The Special One

One pear
wrapped in gold
among the common
mottled green.

We ate
our Christmas bounty
one by one,
the golden fruit
unchosen
until the last,

but it had spoiled.

Conversation

The wind
and bamboo
are tussling
today

One blows
one bends
One lifts
one lowers

Both knock
against my
window

As I read
I hear
scratches

snatches
of conversation

The wind
boasts
of its force

The bamboo
holds fast

deeply rooted
it whispers

the wind
is only
passing through

Between Seasons

From my high window
dried stalks in the bamboo,
bare, unbending.

A dead branch of oak
spans the deck below.
Green leaves open
on yellow forsythia,
cherry trees bloom.

White dogwood blossoms.
Violets, grape hyacinth
purple the new grass.

My gaze returns
to the bent and barren branch
waiting to be cut.

Spring Magic

In spring, as kids, we took a magic walk
winding through forsythia. Each clasping
a pebble chosen with great care, we stepped
into the burst of blooms, chanting our wishes.

Spring greeted me this morning with a dazzle
of yellow forsythia low in the yard,
clusters of white cherry blossoms above,
last week's early daffodils still vibrant.

I marvel at forsythia, its resistance
to restraint. Whips reach up, or out, or cross
each other, curving toward moist earth to root.
Shaping forsythia spoils its sprightliness.
Like wishes made in early spring, it needs
sun, good air, and boundless space to flower.

The Dance

The bamboo sways,
dips ever so slightly,
touches the nearest stem,
bows. Then it rests

waiting for the music
of the next breeze.

Listening Still

And Again

Paul, I call him.
Not his name,
but I like it.

Paul, I'm lost.

He sits down
and starts again,
from the beginning.

Snapshot

I can still picture sitting by the phone,
photo album on my lap, camera ready,
ashtray filled with half-smoked cigarettes,
candy wrappers crumpled on the floor.

The receiver squatted on its base,
the black cord a coiled umbilicus.
A week before a voice—had it once counted
my fingers and toes?—broke through 18 years.

Finally. We walk toward each other, wordless,
hesitate, hug. She's a full head shorter,
young enough to be my sister. In day's light
an old image begins to fade.

We bend over the open book. Her eyes
fix on the wide-eyed infant, head
newly raised. She smiles at the baby
beaming into a floor-length mirror,

just glances at a toddler in footed p.j.'s,
a clown prancing in a pre-school parade, a masked
princess. Does she notice the budding beneath
the ballerina's pink leotard, the graduation grin?

She returns to the beginning, picks up
a clearly focused four-month old,
a print she'll keep. I ask to take her picture.
No, please, she says, *I'm camera shy.*

When I look at these pages now,
my eye is drawn to the empty square
like the tongue to a missing tooth.
The negative is put away, somewhere.

I Stepped on a Crack

I broke my mother's back when I was born.
No, not then. Then she stayed in bed, and cried a lot.
I made her sick.

When I was little, I didn't know it
but that was when I broke my mother's back.
She turned to yell at me, and fell down the stairs.

She never picked me up again. But I have a secret
power. I keep it hidden. I can even
make you blind, if I want to.

Now I'm this many ... one, two, three.
Then I'll be four. I wish someone
would pick me up. Nobody can. Or maybe

they don't want to. Because I'm so bad.
I'm full of poison. I could poison you.
Or make you dead, like the goldfish

they flushed down the toilet.
I make Nanny keep the stopper in the tub
so I don't go down, too.

People are always telling me *Alice, speak up,
don't swallow your words.* But words
have secrets ... they make me strong.

Maybe if I throw up the stuff
that makes me do bad things,
you will hear me.

Son

Slight, even for six
he stands there,
spindle-legged, mute,

a wisp of hair
gathered behind, the promise
of a ponytail.

He hasn't said a word
all week, since a visit
to his grandma.

Don't call her 'Mom'
the old woman had said.
She's just a witch
your father married.
Your mother's in the ground,
been there since you were born.

He ran from her,
hid in the brush. Police
brought him home.

This morning, again,
he stares at me, silent.
Finally his eyes soften.

Folding himself
into my arms, he whispers,
Mom.

Another Song

For years you sat listening
so carefully to all those
who came to you for help.
Now you stare straight ahead,
unblinking, your face puffy —
all those pills. Your head
doesn't turn.

Yet, you seem to grasp
all that is said. At times
one word bursts out,
entering the conversation
dead-center. Or you respond
You betcha, or, *that's wonderful,*
to what has just been said.
You never fail to say *I love you,*
and later, *please come back.*

Your lack of fluent speech,
robs us of your thoughts and ribald humor.
You used to notice every double-entendre,
and a *purse* was never just a *purse*.
On the phone, yesterday, we sang together,
Happy Birthday and *Row, Row, Row Your Boat,*
getting louder and louder with each refrain.

Friends, surprised how aware you are,
wonder if that's a blessing
or a curse. I think you prefer knowing.
You always have ... or
another song.

Listening Still

I hear you
though I don't speak.

Your stories
become part of me.

Please keep telling
them to me.

Ready, My Love

Each dawn
brings an end
to fitful sleep, silent
moaning of bones.
Pills to ease pain
fog my mind.

I stumble
to the door.
My legs may fail.
My bruised hand
brushes the wall,
sheds skin.
Each breath
a snake hissing
through the house.

There are moments.
Yesterday, Mia
skipped in chattering
about a snowman
she and Sam had made.
Her voice bounced
from the blur
of her face.
I could tell
she did not believe
I had ever swept
arms and legs
on snow.

I am so tired, my love.
The air around me thins,
loses its way.
I hope you understand.

I have made
angels.

Good Night, My Love

It is bedtime.
All day I have avoided
what was on the page,
unwritten.
I wanted to answer
your final poem
but it kept transforming
into my own last poem,
one I'm not ready
to write.

The eye-doctor says
my optic nerve
is healthy enough
for the years I have;
the dentist says
my implants will last.
The cancer is there
but slow-growing.
My doctor says
something else
will kill me.

Unlike you, my love,
I draw breath
freely. I miss you
each day, and try
to understand.

We've had
so much.

Therapy

It seems you have a story hard to tell,
the middle is the place you choose to start.
It's never easy but it might go well.

The silence speaks. Your eyelids swell
and shut. I wait, I listen, do my part.
It seems you have a story hard to tell.

It means revisiting your hidden self
to stumble in the thick and cloying dark.
It's never easy but it might go well.

We've all been there, and I know too well
how one can struggle and still fall apart.
It's true your story is so hard to tell.

You have come to face that which befell
you, to see and feel those deeply buried marks.
It isn't easy but it's going well.

Here, in a way we never could foretell,
we wove connective tissue in our hearts.
I knew you had a story hard to tell.
It was not easy. I hope you will be well.

Time Shifts

Retrieval

Ten years ago she died. This morning
I could not recall her name, no matter
how hard I tried. It was lost somewhere
inside the labyrinth of my brain.
I could recall long lunches, bunches
of flowers she brought, books we bought
to share, times we spent at beaches.

For hours, today, I sought her hidden name.
Later, unbidden, it came to me, clear
and calm and confident, *Pat.* I welcomed
her with joy, and a hint of dread. Not of the dead,
but sensing I could lose my past, bit by bit.
I recited, from memory, "Spring and Fall",
a poem by Gerard Manley Hopkins,

stumbling only where I always have.

Girlfriends

When we first met, it seemed of no great moment.
Soon, I looked for you to smile me into morning
each school day. There was no question
we'd find a way to forge a bit of freedom.
We found a niche where we could smoke in secret,
a coughing, smarting start to our long friendship.

Dailyness developed into a friendship
I treasure up to this very moment.
At first, we giggled, shared what was so secret,
phoned each other first thing in the morning.
We dated twins, giving us some freedom
to postpone the looming *what's next?* question.

Perhaps we feared the answer to that question
would threaten the endurance of our friendship,
knowing we'd no longer have the freedom
to share the mood and madness of each moment.
We pledged there'd never be a morning
we were needed and held back—it was no secret.

There were of course some things we each kept secret.
Our families, our careers, were without question
what filled our thoughts on waking every morning;
our daily chores, our lives full of new friendship.
Still, at times, there'd be a sudden moment
when memories were stirred with easy freedom.

Our bodies no longer have their youthful freedom
to move with ease. Our pain, our aches, a secret
we keep from those around us every moment
to avoid their wearing worry and their questions.
It's only in our lasting life-long friendship
that we can share the dailyness of mourning.

I phoned to hear your voice this very morning,
to laugh together in that welcome freedom
formed by years of deepened friendship.
I do not need to keep from you the secret
that answers have all turned into questions;
that we marvel, muddle, through our moment.

There is a moment early in the morning
when questions, *dream? memory?* mix with freedom.
Distinct and clear—no secret—is our friendship.

Time Shifts

In the room green numbers glow,
change in a blink. I miss the steady
sweep of time, hands slowly circling
the large dial centered on the wall, ruling
my schoolroom, my mother's kitchen.
Now, change comes without warning.

Yesterday I called. *I'm still alive*, you joked.
Today, no answer. I find you
on the floor, eyes empty, cheeks gray.
I cover your sprawled limbs, smooth
your thin hair, make that final call.
And wait, while time shifts.

Your Kitchen

hungers
to be used again.

The table still covered
with oilcloth you chose.
Stained now.
Copper pans, hanging
on hooks in the
exposed brick, coated
with dust.
Dozens of spice-jars,
outdated.
Your mother's
Dutch cabinet,
empty.

I fill the unfed
grinder with black
peppercorns, scrub
and season an iron fry-pan
for my morning omelet.
I choose among
the handmade mugs
a shape to cradle
my coffee, find
a blue-glazed bowl
for fruit, wash out
a brittle roach.

A Single Life

In third grade, you gave me a locket with your picture.
Round as a teddy bear, I loved you.

Michelangelo had David, at thirteen I had you. In my dreams.
All summer I watched you on the pier, your every move.

Dad saw your picture in the paper, my prom date, not Jewish.
He said I could not go. The forfeit, college. I went to both.

A college weekend, my first. A snow festival. Two innocents,
groped and groping on the bottom of a bunk bed.

In grad school, you told me it would get easier, over time, to bear
the pain of life. You held me.

We met on a leisurely crossing to England, met again, as planned,
in Italy, islanded on Ischia, hitchhiked in Greece. The sunset at
Sounion, Maria Callas at Epidaurus. Only later I guessed that
you were gay.

The boat trip back, I met a very smart sabra. Out of the blue, he
proposed. That was dumb.

At the office, we talked endlessly. Your wife was pregnant. You
said you loved me. I changed jobs.

I loved your body. And the way you called me *sweetness*.
You satisfied my lust, for a while. You met my friends, I met few
of yours. I was shocked when you married.

We made love on the couch. At campsites. In tents.
In motels. Had high tea in Victoria. Great wine saved for Banff.
At the end, I would have married you.

No, I said, resisting your embrace. *I love you both too much.* I
knew we'd three be sorry when she came home.

I see you each year at Kim's New Year's party, with wife and
daughter. I see your lingering look. I just couldn't bring myself
to marry you, you were so proper.

You were both on the faculty. I babysat. We kept in touch,
visited ... one year she stayed behind, your hug turned insistent.
It would have felt like incest.

A secret. I moved here for you. I loved your rust hair, your
freckles, your ease with tough kids at camp. You anointed my
body with scotch, drank me in before entering. This was what I
came for.

A blanket of snow would mean you'd spend the night.

You would come to town, unannounced. You never slowed
down. I always welcomed you ... until I met him.

I remember my parents' friend, Beatrice, paralyzed from the
waist down. Ben always there, pushing her, lifting her,
loving her.

Frogs

I had to kiss many a frog
before I found a prince,
my friend said.

I have kissed my share,
more than,
but they were not
transformed.

I always stepped back
a distance
to view the dark green skin
and bulging eyes
of an amphibian.

Postscript

I found a prince
in my back yard.
I kissed him,
he awoke. I was
transformed.

At the Movies

We were early, easy parking,
no ticket line, *two seniors, please,*
and a hearing device for me.
We sat near the back, alone
in the theater. Your lips found mine,
our tongues touched. With your hand
on my thigh, my body pulsed awake.
My hand brushed your gray beard,
tingling my fingertips. You tasted
each finger that fondled your lips;
your hand cupped my breast.
Discreet, we made sure no one
was coming. *This is why teenagers*
go to drive-ins, I whispered.
As others arrived, we held hands,
knowing we had a place
to build a fire.

A Proposal

You greet me with your lips,
link my arm in yours,
awaken sleeping senses.
I thought such moments
forever past. I dream again
of being joined, of joying.

We do not have much time,
dear friend, to thrust
and parry. Nor would I
marry. But I welcome
you within, and hold you
close, come what may.

No Complaints

Divine, you whispered
this morning, tasting the nipple
of my left breast.

When we find each other
again, as we did last night,
I press to feel our every molecule.
Dos, our aging cat, mews for room.

This bed once felt
the shudders and quakes
of youth, now enjoys tremors
of spreading pleasure.

I walk through the house
remembering a kitchen in Provence,
suffused with the yellow of sun
and just a touch of blue.

afterwards
our bodies curve together …
so fitting

my arm moves …
our shifting bodies
entwine the night

you left with the sun …
I watch the waning light
my eyes grow tired

Choices

Will I come with you?
Your hands, weeding the garden,
have loosened the clotted ground.

Are you coming soon?
There are plants to be watered
and the cat waits to be fed.

The Shasta Daisies

we bought last week
are radiant this fogged-in
morning, each stem tall
in a plastic sleeve.

We found a clear pitcher
to set them in, framed
by the picture window
with the bullet-hole.

Today I trimmed them,
hoping they would last
another day or two.

Shorter each year,
we sheathe each other
until the final cut.

You Walk Away

You walk me to my car,
watch me lift myself in,
turn and walk toward
your neighbor's house.

I watch your back.
You look so frail,
balding between graying
strands, footsteps careful.

You turn my way again,
watch my U-turn, blow
a kiss, and walk away,
a moment like many others.

This time, the sun has set.
Still, there is a shadow.

Mirrors

Last night you dreamed us back
to when our pulses quickened.
Do you remember my body then?
You tell me, this morning,
that I am beautiful.
You do not seem to see the bumps,
the blemishes, the bruises.
You are a more forgiving mirror
than the one on my door, the one
that reflects my mother's furrowed face,
splotched skin, sagging breasts.
Her eyes had clouded over.
Mine are still clear.

your voice
still answers—
five years after

Far From Home

On Hearing Stanley Kunitz Read
His Translation of Paul Celan's Todesfuge,
(Deathfugue), at the U.S. Holocaust Memorial
Museum, 4/17/02

He leans, for a moment,
on a woman's arm.
Bent and frail, using his cane,
he ascends alone.

His strong, clear voice
etches a poem
into our memory.

Shower Rooms

We women of a certain age straggle from the pool,
shed suits, rinse off chlorine. I gaze at the array
of breasts, small and firm, round and full, drooping.
None so thin, so pendulous, as were my mother's.

And those others, in the steam room
at Brighton Beach. I waited eagerly to board
the train, to reach, at last, a place to brave
the waves, to bury my brother in sand.

But first I was tethered to my aunts,
there in that hidden room, where old women,
cleansing their pores, told secrets in strange tongues.
Warm mist clouded their wrinkled flesh. I shrank.

It was 1939. So much I did not know.
I did not know to witness.
I did not know to welcome.
I did not understand the language of survival.

Far From Home

... the cavalrymen ... dined on gazelle ...*

A lone gazelle, grazing near the grapes.
You have escaped the cheetah
in the wilds of Africa, been pictured
leaping in the marshy heavens,
eluding the lion.
Such gentle grace.

Here, prancing in the palace
compound, you were always
endangered; the vine-covered walls
contained you for the hunting party
of the dictator and his guests.
Such grace.

After liberation, a marksman's bullet
is placed to spare you pain.
Fawn colored coat,
white underbelly exposed.
His hand grasps your thin hind legs,

drags you on the ground, your dark
eyes forever darkened. You
will be skinned with a keen edge,
flanks hacked with accuracy,
stewed to perfection.

Our weary soldiers,
craving home,
will say grace.

*Washington Post 5/29/2003.

97

Bombs Bursting

How did I carry you,
my wondrous child,
ten fingers, ten toes?

How do I soothe you,
my fretful babe?
Nuzzle with me, sleep.

How will I bury you
my silent child?
Bathe your body and
cover you with earth.

For Country

It is a strange war.

Those of us who have
spend more and more.
Others are asked

to spend their lives,
even before their seed

is spent.

See Also: Spare

In reserve,
easily done
without.

In the wards,
now, spare parts
for limbs lost,
unspared,

irreplaceable.

Soldiers
(A found poem)*

Soldiers might be able
to fix a broken-down
Humvee on the battlefield
so it won't be left
for scavengers, but a soldier
showing signs of mental stress
or mental breakdown
in a hostile environment
may be out of luck.

*The National Psychologist, 1/2007, article by Richard E. Gill

Round About

Queens in the Garden

After King and Queen, by Henry Moore, and *Seated Yucatan Woman,* by Francisco Zuniga. Hirshhorn Museum and Sculpture Garden, Smithsonian Institution, Washington, DC.

The king and queen,
slim bodies of bronze,
perch on a curving bench.
How can they be so weightless,
so unmarked, the queen's slight
nipples the only sign of sex?
Single eyed, they stare into space,
neither sees the other.
They do not deign to speak.

Further down the path

the woman from the Yucatan
is seated on a camp chair, her legs
spread wide under a broad draped skirt,
her massive bronze body at ease.
Her eyes are closed, her face smooth.
She has already loved, given birth,
nursed, grieved. Now she rests.
When you can, be still, she says.
When you must, be fierce.

Ghazal

These babes have been given their lives for one day.
Such innocence only survives for one day.

In darkness we live and in darkness we toil.
The north sun our landscape revives for one day.

The journey is over, the deathbed is made.
The prodigal daughter arrives, for one day.

This striated sky, surf-drawn ridges in sand
provide much delight to our eyes, for one day.

The families are gathered, the lovers are wed.
Men, women, and children imbibe, for one day.

The song they are singing, all voices joined in
is offered to us, a reprise, for one day.

A new day is coming, let's dance into dawn.
We Small ones are earthbound, we thrive for one day.

Landscapes

The dune is silent.
Bent only on being,
no need to be seen.

On our wall, a scene
framed, contained,
awaiting a viewer.

Lost Words

At the Dada exhibit
at the National Gallery of Art
memories of lost lives,
lost limbs, lost meaning.
And directions by Tristan Tzara
how to make a Dadaist poem.

In today's news, an 18-year-old
ambushes a police station
with seven loaded guns.
Shoots and maims and kills
until gunned down.

I cut out each of the words
from the newspaper article,
put them into a plastic bag,
carry them upstairs.

When ready to let them
fall onto the page
I cannot find them.
Misplaced.
as is so much.

Someday I may find
a bag of words, and wonder
whose they are.

DaDa, D.C. 2006

Blanketed, grateful for shoulders
explaining mortally of delusions
settled and silence
walked the seven over the rage near police.
But a day loaded have shoot, pulled
as a cruiser and shotguns.
Flowers, officer with and but passion slung roses
stood the gates from police outside
parked guy came eighteen emerge bullets
the detectives, those on reason
mums pieces without final
fired more for troubled lilies
to struck all cars of wounding officers
every died on public fence
in that down station with him
guns many all end his of
and the police of the rest.
If his home piled up the down times.

David Kirby In My Head

I'm at the refreshment table at the Library of Congress
          having just heard a poetry reading by David Kirby
and Li-Young Lee, a poet whose work I have loved ever since
          a suitor sent me a copy of *From Blossoms* when we were
first courting and he thought the sensuality would speak to me,
          which it did, but he did not; it seemed a prior girlfriend
had sent it to him, but I am grateful to him for the introduction
          to these poems and feel like I have been at a feast tonight

not only for the delicious sounds—and sight—of Li-Young Lee
          who is really gorgeous with dark hair and such deep eyes,
but also for the extensive narratives related with much humor
          and ultimately sly wisdom by David Kirby, a poet
whose work I did not know but found fascinating to listen to.
          So I am spearing asparagus into the creamy dip
and picking up skewers of broiled salmon that can be dipped

into soy sauce and chatting with my friend Patsy about the virtues
          of freecycling at the same time that I am watching the line
of readers clutching newly purchased books and inching
          their way to Li-Young Lee's signing table where
an efficient member of the staff is asking people's names
          and writing them down for the poet, which not only helps
to get the spelling right but also saves his voice, which was strained
          this evening, as he had such a bad cold but he persevered

as Patsy does in asking me about freecycling—
          she seems more interested in free food and how to get
free goods than in the poetry. Actually she's here
          mainly to get a ride home as she works nearby and lives
on my block and I don't mind as I really don't like walking
          to the car by myself so I tell her about how I gave away
twelve lectures on existentialism from *The Teaching Company*

that I got as a 2-fer when I requested a series of lectures
        on the history of the English language, that I may actually
listen to in my car, which, like me, is old enough
        to have a tape player, yet I know I will never
listen to tapes on existentialism—I have enough trouble
        with the meaning of poems in the *New Yorker*—so I offer
them on Freecycle and get two responses, but not one
        complete sentence. Not that I mind run-on sentences

but one said only, *I need to expand my metal horizons…*
        write me if it's free, leaving me a picture of metal
stretched by the idea that Freecycle items are, indeed,
        free. I have a strong preference to respond to requests
when I'm not tempted to correct the spelling or content
        unless the writer is not a native English speaker,
in which case I often feel great admiration especially

as I can hardly speak a clear and direct sentence
        in any of the foreign languages I've studied and studied
but have not learned. In my late twenties, I was in Mexico
        and bought a set of dishes in an open market and wanted
to ask for something to ship them in, armed with a Spanish
        phrase-book and 4 years of high-school Latin, including
the year in which our fourth year Latin teacher, Miss Popper,
        who lived with Miss Bales, always called on Billy Goldstein

to translate the purple passages as his cheeks would slowly
        suffuse with blush; Billy and I were the only two juniors
in a class full of seniors who snickered when Billy stammered
        and also seemed to share some knowledge of our teacher's private
life that was outside the realm of my limited knowledge, so now
        I tried to improvise, after asking *donde puedo encontrar*
I made up a word for "carton," and met the same kind of snickers

as Billy had, and only later when I took a course
    did I realize I had asked for *cojones*, balls, which
in a way is what I had making up words like that.
    Finally the line has dwindled, and I tell Li-Young Lee
how much I like his poems, and ask him if he would sign
    the books I brought with me, and he is gracious and inscribes,
Fellow flower, let's keep opening, in his book entitled
    Rose, and it's not until later that I make the connection

and Patsy asks me about the other response to my offer
    of tapes, and I tell her the second, *I'll take it. Where?* was even
worse and less related to anything; but I have had time
    to reflect that we all do our best to be understood and don't
always make the right connections so I gave the tapes to the guy
    who didn't proofread and was not sure what to believe but knew
that he, like all of us, needed some metal exercise.

While We Slept

The tooth fairy came for her change.
Pumpkins glowered in the dark.
Who's that sleeping with Papa Bear?
Apple catalogue: seeds of sin, seven varieties.
The rains from heaven have not been gentle.
What did you see in this dawn's early light?
Blinded voters were hiding in the bush.
Brave men took to the hills.
Hearing aids lay screaming on the table.
Don't touch the wired fence along the roadside!
No more playing paper, scissors, rockets.
Can we play hide and seek? Blind man's bluff?
You're either with us or against us.
Close your eyes tight, be invisible.

Round About

Wandering around the old fair grounds
I fall into a cavernous pit
land on a gray speckled horse
moving up and down on a shiny pole
as the platform beneath it turns.
The third time around I grab the brass ring
swing onto a tree growing out of the wall
as three mystic monkeys call my name,
cast out all evil, and give me
the silver key I need
to enter the final maze.
The merry-go-round never stops.

No Eye

no ego, no speaker
no center, no core
no room for sorrow
or joy, or humor

ears, nose, mouth and throat
arms, legs, hands and feet
arches, toes, and knees
knuckles, chest, and breasts
shoulders, neck, and head
eyebrows, teeth, and cheeks

an ovary or two
heartbeats to measure
no hang-ups, no *am*
no *was*, no *become*
no *now*, no *then*

unaware, untold
no start, no stop
no release, no end
no ever
no ...

Turtle Rush

Turtle sinks teeth
into heroin
is what I read
in this morning's *Post.*

How long
had the turtle
been waiting
for a rush?
I named him
De Quincey,
as in *Thomas.*

I picked up
the paper, read
it again. This time
it said *heron,*
as in *blue.*

Yellow Cheese

I won't.
I can't.
I'll do what
I want.
I'll stand still
And chant.
I'll eat
What I please
No carrots
No peas
Just yellow cheese.
I'll push food
Off my plate
Spill milk
On the floor
Pull doggie's tail
Run out the door.
I'll clap my hands
To make you smile
I'm glad I am
Your only child.

Nursery Rhyme

There was an old woman
who lived in a shoe,
something all in D.C. knew.
What were we supposed to do?

Not me, said the housing inspector,
I don't examine shoes.
But if the laces are not frayed
consider that good news.

Not me, said the social worker,
spanking is not abuse.
And when we said the kids aren't fed
she still remained obtuse.

Not me, said the homeroom teacher,
they never come to school.
I know when not to interfere,
I'm sure nobody's fool.

Not me, said the sports director,
they'd overrun my teams.
I'm sure they'd never learn the rules,
besides, they're not too clean.

Not me, said the local doctor,
I can't see them for free.
I've all the patients I can treat,
what do you want from me?

The parish priest, a man of God,
said Sunday I will bless them.
And if they are of age to come
I'll hear each one's confession.

The old woman had only her shoe,
it stood there in plain sight.
She gathered all the children in,
then pulled the laces tight.

Minding One's p's and q's

My pulse quickens. Put to the quest
I'm pursuing the quickest
path to queerness.
Not a party, not a quinceañera
not a political rally of questionable value.
Please. Please. Question, question, question.
You were taught to mind your p's and q's
say please and thankq
to not confuse the p's and q's when setting type.
(Why not mind your b's and d's?
my mirror asks.)
Oh, yes, that mirror
says no, not pretty, a bit quirky-looking,
but what the hell ... you've already had too many pints
and quarts,
are quarrelsome and pouty—
oops, I've mixed up the p's and q's
how quaintly perfect.
I'm sure you never mistook a pence for a quid,
a penny for a quarter,
a pineapple for a quince—so, what's the point?
That is precisely the question.

.

?

Weather Report

The current temperature
is not available.
Please try again later.

We've been warned
of global warming,
the coming floods

but not of air
no temperature
at all. No scale

to measure what's
not there. *Not available*
is what she said
when I dialed
the weather forecast
on my upstairs phone

first thing this morning,
all windows closed.
I threw on some clothes

rushed downstairs
to step outside.
To my relief

I felt a chill.

Time Flies

I walk down 95th Street carrying
my parking meter. The curb is crowded
with parked cars. There's no place
to put it.

I want to board the bus on 96th Street
but have to pay a parking meter first.
I brought my own, since it's so hard
to find one.

I decide to swim across the park.

The mime on the museum steps
takes off his invisible watch,
throws it away, and invites me
to dance.

A Riddle

I have rocked and rocked
The world remains un-ruled.

On The Bus

The hand of the child
so small, with tiny nails,
curled exquisitely in sleep,

the father's body firm
against his drowsing son

who stirs, then stands.
His intense gaze takes in
the world, piece by piece.

Why I Write

I write to sense the sound
of my own breath, to hear
even the silences.

Acknowledgements

I thank the editors of the following publications in which some of these poems, or versions thereof, first appeared: *Beltway Poetry Quarterly, District Lines, The Federal Poet, The Glover Park Gazette, Poets on the Fringe,* and *Prospectus...A Literary Offering*

I want to thank my colleagues in the Federal Poets and in the Poets on the Fringe workshops for their support and helpful critiques.

I thank Laura Brown, Herb Guggenheim, Anne Garner, and Gwenn Gebhard for their careful reading of this manuscript, and their many thoughtful comments. Thanks to Lee Giesecke for his careful attention to the haiku. I am grateful to Ellie Heginbotham, Miles David Moore, and Karl O'Hanlon for their close reading and reviews of these poems.

I appreciate the help of Michael Price and Victor Benitez of the Digital Commons staff of the D.C. Public Library in designing and formatting this book. I am especially grateful to Jayanthi Sambasivan and the rest of staff of the Georgetown Neighborhood Library of the D.C. Public Library for all their help and support.

Special thanks go to Rosalie Werback for her continuing help and support as well as her invaluable assistance with the book design.

And I am most indebted to my loving partner, Mel Kohn, for his constant support. While he is not unbiased, I take delight in his enthusiasm for my work.

Edna Small grew up in Passaic, New Jersey and now resides in Washington D.C. She graduated from Antioch College in Yellow Springs, Ohio, then earned a Ph.D. in Psychology from the University of Michigan. With a lifelong love of poetry, she read widely and wrote an occasional poem. Since retiring from a very satisfying career as a clinical psychologist, she has devoted herself to the study and writing of poetry. This collection of poems written in the last fifteen years celebrates her 85th birthday.

29697202R00094

Made in the USA
Middletown, DE
28 February 2016